GOD ONLY KNOWS

GOD STILL KNOWS

MORE POEMS ABOUT LIFE, LOVE, FAMILY, SCHOOL, HOPE AND GOD

CLAUS RANSWILL

Copyright © Claus Ranswill 2020
ISBN: 9798677656040
Imprint: Independently published

No part of this publication may be reproduced, stored in a retrieval system, or transmitted in any form or by any means – electronic, mechanical, digital photocopy, recording, or any other without the prior permission of the author.

All rights Reserved solely by the author. The author guarantees all contents are original and do not infringe upon the legal rights of any other person or work. The views expressed in this book are not necessarily those of the publisher.

TABLE OF CONTENTS:

6	RECOMMENDATIONS BY FELLOW WORLDLY POETS:
7	INTRODUCTION / PREFACE
9	BELIEVE
10	EDUCATION
12	EMOTIONAL INTELLIGENCE
13	A VALENTINES DAY POEM
14	AS LONG AS FOREVER
15	CAN YOU FEEL THIS FEELING?
16	CAN'T WE GET ALONG
17	WHEN
18	MY BIRTHDAY
19	BEAUTIFUL ANGEL
20	THE MOST INFLUENCIAL
21	MY MOM HAS BREAST CANCER
23	MY AUNT JUST DIED
25	MY IN LAWS
27	GENERATIONS
28	MOTHERHOOD
29	GRANDMOTHERS
30	A STAY AT HOME MOM
32	LITTLE JOYS IN MY LIFE
33	FAMILY
34	AARON
35	JOSHUA
36	KIRSTEN
37	FISHING AT SALTON SEA
38	THE LIBRARY
40	CALLING CENTER BLUES
42	THE MENTALLY ILL
43	SPENDAHOLIC
44	THE OTHER DAY
45	JOY
46	PROLIFIC
47	MY OBSESSION
48	WHY THE RHYME
49	WAR OF WORDS
50	CREATIVITY
51	RELEASE

52	A MILLION THINGS
53	MEMORIES
54	CONVOLUTED
55	THE DAY SLIPPED AWAY
56	THE OTHER DAY I STOPPED
57	ALWAYS LATE
58	ALWAYS CRITICAL
59	ANOTHER POEM ABOUT T.V.
60	ANOTHER VACATION
61	ANOTHER DAY INTO THE FUTURE
62	ANOTHER BASEBALL GAME
63	ANOTHER DAY ANOTHER FIGHT
64	ANOTHER DAY FUTURE'S GONE
65	ANOTHER FIGHT
66	ANOTHER BEAUTIFUL DAY
67	A LESSON I'VE LEARNED IN LIFE
68	ANOTHER LESSON I'VE LEARNED IN LIFE
69	A DREAM COME TRUE
70	TWENTY-FOUR HOURS
71	DREAM VACATION
72	DREAMING
73	MY SPECIAL PLACE
74	THE LIVING ROOM
75	BIRTH SCHOOL WORK DEATH
76	DEATH
77	LOOK AT GODS BEAUTY
78	ANTS
79	THE LAWN
80	THE WIND
81	WAVE WATCHING
82	PEACE
83	PEACE, LOVE AND HAPPINESS
84	DESTINY
86	IT AINT OVER
87	THE INTERNET
88	ARMED FORCES
89	FOOD
90	THREE SISTERS
91	BOUNCE
92	A CRAZY WORLD
93	YOU ARE SO VAIN
94	THE END IS NEAR
95	THE MOON GLIDING THROUGH THE NIGHT

96	A Poem inspired by a suggestion from Joni Russo COLORFUL CANVAS IN THE SKY
98	A Poem inspired from a Jeff King photo IT TOOK ME MANY YEARS TO LET GO. I FINALLY LET GO AND IT WAS TOO LATE... A Poem inspired by a suggestion from Janice Parham Jesson
100	IF I COULD ONLY WRITE, I WOULD WRITE YOU A SONG A Poem inspired by a suggestion from Debbie Gatlin
101	CANCER TOOK THE LOVE OF MY LIFE A Poem Suggestion from Eric Huttar
103	THE EARTH CRIES OUT FOR HUMANITY A Poem inspired by a suggestion from Ntwanano Mashele
104	IF ALL POETS WROTE THE SAME WHAT BORING POEMS THEY WOULD BE A Poem inspired by a suggestion from Lance Armstrong-Robinson
106	MY GIFT FROM GOD THE POEM AND WRITING
108	LOW SELF ESTEEM
110	MAKING NEW FRIENDS EVERY DAY
112	WHAT DOES IT FEEL LIKE TO BE NUMBER ONE?
113	HOW DO I MAKE MONEY WITH MY WORDS?
114	DOES THE WORLD REALLY NEED ANOTHER POET?
115	CLAUS IN THE HOUSE
116	THE MORE I WRITE
118	GOD ALMIGHTY

RECOMMENDATIONS BY FELLOW WORLDLY POETS:

"Claus' Rhymes opens our eyes to our humanness: the words stand simple yet run deep into our emotions, how we struggle in our hearts, in our homes, at school and at our work places, and how faith works a way out for us, for God Still Knows. It is a Poetry Collection worthy reading."
Geoffrey Esilima, author of THE 7 WOMEN PLUS, THE LOST WORLDS, JOY & HAPPINESS (three poetry collections published on Amazon Kindle)

"Claus Ranswill has written another great book entitled "God Still Knows" which is full of simple and brilliant rhymes and poems. It is an emotional roller coaster journey that takes the reader through a life of ups and downs about family, school, work, love and pain, that we all can relate to. This is his second book and he will have a long bright future as an accomplished poet and writer. I can't wait to see his upcoming works of art; I am sure they will also be great."
Jack Tomlinson, author of "Behind the Mask" which can be found on amazon https://www.amazon.com/Behind-Mask-Jack-Tomlinson-ebook/dp/B0888WJ1FD

INTRODUCTION / PREFACE

Once again before I begin, I have to thank my lord and savior Jesus Crist for saving me and giving me the strength to survive and for giving me the gift to write poems that saved my life. These poems tell stories of everyday situations. I have to thank my beautiful wife Debbie for standing by my side through thick and thin for the past 38 years dating and marriage. I want to thank all my children Aaron, Joshua, and Kirsten, my In Laws, my mom and dad all my extended brothers and sisters, Lance, Jason, Craig, Valerie and Gail. I would also like to thank my brother Steven and any extended family on my wife's side, there are way too many to thank individually.

These poems are a continuation from my first book God Only Knows. This book contains around 60 or so poems from 2000 and around 20 or so from 2001-2008 that I wrote while going to college and written during different periods of work, life, stress, enjoying nature and love. It also contains around 15 or so brand-new ones that were written this year 2020 from suggestions and other inspirations from Facebook as I was promoting my first book God Only Knows and also attending church and a new poem that touches on the stupid virus we are all suffering the effects of today as I put this book together. This is a happier mixture of my poems and a more organized compilation unlike my last book in which I was overwhelmed and picked 100 out of a huge variety from the year 2000.

Many of these poems were written due to assignments from college English classes, and suggestions by friends, relatives and Facebook friends. Some were reflections of past family memories, and observations from my work environments. Just like my first book, many of these poems were written during a tremendous amount of life stress including a foreclosure, repossession of our car, moving back in with my in-laws, and trying to focus on all the homework of college while receiving 3 AA's in 3 and a half years.

If you liked my first book, God Only Knows, you will love this book. This is the second book with many more books on the way.

I am currently working on a third book of poems, a haiku book, a children's book and a biography. I have a lot of words in my brain and I should be able to finish these real soon. Please keep an eye out on social media for any updates and new poems I may write before my next book comes out. I am also a life insurance agent in California and can give out free quotes over the phone.

You can find me on social media on the following links

Personal website: https://ranswill.com/
Facebook: https://www.facebook.com/ranswill
Twitter: https://twitter.com/ClausRanswill
Instagram: https://www.instagram.com/cranswill/
Email: cranswill@hotmail.com
Phone: 760-574-7096

BELIEVE

The sun, the moon, the sky above
The grass, the trees, the one I love

The wind, the water, the earth below
A stranger walking by with a friendly hello

The birds, the cats, the dogs and fish
You can have anything that you wish

Don't be afraid the sky is the limit
Shoot for the stars then you will win it

All of your dreams and all your desires
Are stronger than all of Satan's hell fires

Don't take my word for it, try it and see
You can have everything you want,
if you just
        BELIEVE.

EDUCATION

C.O.D. and ROP,
    both of these have been quite a treat,
with the new teachers and other students
    that I had to meet.
It was hard at first; I didn't know a thing,
but now it is time, for me to celebrate and sing.

It's gotten easier as the weeks went on by.
Now the classes are over, how fast the time did fly.
Almost time for a degree, just a year and half remain,
then I can get on with my life and be driving in the fast lanes.

Computer skills are the future,
    that's what I've been taking,
because it seems my whole life,
    all I've been doing is faking.
Everywhere I've worked and all the skills I've had,
are nothing compared to
    what I have now, I am so glad.

Everything happens for a reason,
    I know that now for sure,
but just a few years ago,
    I didn't think there was a cure,
for this life that I had been living, in pure misery,
has turned around and now my life is full of tranquility.

I can't help but write poems, almost every day.
This is something, that would never had happened,
if not for that fateful and unforgettable,
    September day
when my boss at the time,
    tried so hard to make my life flatten.

It has been a treat; all the teachers have been so kind.
I wish that I had listened, back eighteen years ago,
when everyone told me to go to college.
I must have been out of my mind,
for not listening and taking everyone's advice.
I guess my mind is just too slow.

Can't think about the past,
    now that the future is up ahead.
I need to stop wishing all those librarians were dead.
They will get what they deserve, time will only tell.
It won't be long,
    before they are all frying in their own hell.

EMOTIONAL INTELLIGENCE

Emotional intelligence, artificial life
Futures moving way too fast causing so much strife

Psychological warfare, emotional distress
Technological future, sometimes more is less

Industrial revolution, came and went so fast
Computer age is here, how long will it last?

Psychological intelligence, emotional warfare
So hard to live our lives in constant despair

Technological warfare, emotional drain
Will not the future drive us all insane?

Emotional revolution, psychological scars
Losing all patience while driving our turbo cars

Psychological warfare, artificial intelligence
There's got to be life out there in all the heavenly skies elegance

Industrial intelligence, robots have replaced
All of the hard workers now they are displaced

A VALENTINES DAY POEM

How do I describe

The love I have for you

With you on my mind,

There's nothing else I need to do

Thoughts of our love,

Together through the years

In all the happy moments

And even through the tears

Our love will last forever

No one will ever sever

Forever it will last

Never will it end

Back and forth between us

We will always send

Our love to each other

Till the end of time

Here's another love poem

With another simple rhyme

Trying to describe the love

That came from up above

AS LONG AS FOREVER

As long as there is blood,
> pumping through my veins.

As long as there is breath,
> filling up my lungs.

Every heartbeat and breath of air,
> you control the reigns.

Our love is like a ladder,
> and you control the rungs.

Every drop of blood,
> every ounce of air.

Every single emotion,
> from love down to despair.

You control my thoughts,
> and every ounce of being.

If not for all my love,
> you would not be seeing.

All of the emotions
> I put to paper from pen.

Without all my love,
> to you, from me, what then?

CAN YOU FEEL THIS FEELING?

Can you feel this feeling?
Deep within my soul.
Love has got me reeling.
I've lost complete control.

Love takes over.
There's nothing I can do.
Like a four-leaf clover.
I'm lucky to be with you.

Can you feel this feeling?
Deep down inside.
Love it is so healing.
No place to run and hide.

Can you feel this feeling?
It feels so wonderful.
Like four aces you are dealing.
And I am on a roll.

Can you feel this feeling?
The feeling I feel for you.
It is so appealing.
I wish you felt it to.

CAN'T WE GET ALONG

Can't we all just get along?
Live another day to sing another song.

Can't we just live in peace and harmony,
Whether we're broke
    or have an abundance of money?

No more fights, no more fury.
Stop living life in such a hurry.

Why the fights, instead of celebration,
So much destruction, instead of jubilation?

What's the point, will mankind ever change?
Or is it just like the buffalo, extinct from the range.

Happiness gone, all that's left is hatred,
For one another, the love is all but dead.

Is it too late to change, do we still have time,
Before JESUS comes back,
    and the earth stops on a dime?

Think about it, before it's too late,
And GOD looks down and becomes too irate.

We cannot last too much longer.
We all need prayer
    to become a little bit more stronger.

WHEN

When is it too late,
    to say I love you?
When is it too late,
    to tell them we are through?
Is it when you think,
    you've run out of things to do?
Is it when you think,
    there's too much left to do?
When will you tell me,
    that you love me too?
When will you leave me ,
    right out of the blue?
Is it when your feelings, for me, you outgrew?
Is it when your anger and hostility just blew?
When will you love me,
    the way I love you?
When will you love me?
    You know the feelings are so true!
Will you ever love me?
    I hope someday you do!
Will you ever love me,
    and never leave me too?
You know you love me!
    You know you feel it too!
You know you love me!
    You love me through and through!
You know you love me!
    There's nothing you can do!
I can feel the love between me and you!

MY BIRTHDAY

Today is my birthday-
    Thirty-six years old
A day like any other day-
    Can I sound so bold?
Never did I think-
    I would see the day
The year two-thousand-
    Come into play
Thoughts of suicide-
    Seemed to vanish in the air
Now every calendar-
    I can't help but stop and stare
I can't believe-
    Time goes by so fast
Where is my childhood?
    Why did it not last?
Never did I save-
    The money that I made
Every penny I spent-
    Every paycheck I was paid
Always buying collectibles-
    For the future just in case
That instead of suicide-
    I would choose life in its place
Then I got married-
    And we had three beautiful children
Now my life has meaning-
    I feel like I'm in heaven!

BEAUTIFUL ANGEL

Beautiful angel sleeping so sound
All children are the same that's what I've found

Angels when asleep
Monsters when awake
Wish that I could keep
All the memories that are at stake

Deep inside my mind ready to recall
Anytime that I need
to remember them
Getting back up after they fall

Beautiful angels all our children are
How we spoil, when we take love too far
Giving them everything, they always want
Always giving in, the spoiled-ness will always haunt

How much love, is too much to give?
How much punishment, will push it too far?
Too bad there's not a parent's handbook
    to help us live
Day by day, whether at home or in the car

Beautiful angels sent from God above
All that we can do, is give them all of our love

THE MOST INFLUENCIAL

The person who has influenced me the most
Has got to be my mom she raised me the most
Besides the characters on all those TV Shows
She was always there for all my highs and lows

Not many role models roaming through my life
A couple of teachers and of course my beautiful wife
TV and rock and roll
      have been the biggest influences on me
Not that they controlled me but molded me into me

It must've been hard for my mother
Raising us by herself, me and my brother
Al least till she married our stepdad
I forget what age we were,
      but I bet she was really glad
Don't ever remember going to church all of my youth
At least not taken by my mom
      `I think I went with other youths
She may not have been perfect,
      but I guess she did the best she could
I don't think she would've changed anything
      even if she could
So, I guess my mom, my wife, and a few teachers too
All had the biggest influence on me,
      to this day they still do
A lot of my impatience
      I think was passed on hereditarily
Maybe it's a copout or maybe
      it's just temporary insanity

MY MOM HAS BREAST CANCER

Breast cancer has attacked my mom
Now radiation has taken her hair
What can I do to help her out
when I am so busy with school and life?

My focus is blurred, and my mind is weak
I try too hard to shelter my problems
I keep it all inside
One day I am going to explode

Cancer is a horrible and dreaded disease
I hope one day there can be a cure
What is the cause and what can be done
To pick her up when she is feeling run down

She still smokes and I don't understand why
She has already lost her sister to cancer
Addiction is stupid and needs to be addressed
Is quitting cold turkey so hard

Do we all reap what we all sow?
Do we all get what we all deserve?
Is cancer a deserved disease
     or something that just happens?

Did the operation get all the cancer
     or will it reoccur later?
Will it spread throughout her body
     and eventually kill her?

Questions that will eventually be addressed
But in the meantime, all we can do is wait and pray
When is the last time you told your mother
     you loved them?
Isn't it about time before it is too late?

To you mom, I love you,
     I know I don't say it often enough
I am sorry that my life got so busy,
     but I thank God you are so tough

MY AUNT JUST DIED

My aunt just died the other day
I am not sure what I can say
Smoking kills, I've said it before
Now she is at heavens front door

Was it caused by her chain smoking?
I'm not saying this just to be joking
About her life, so short it was
About brain cancer and what it does

Her life didn't have to end this way
So much more to life each and every day
Left behind two sons who will miss
Visiting her daily and receiving her kiss

Two local nephews, my brother and me
Will miss the only aunt we have ever known
Who knows what more she was meant to see?
Who knows how much more she could've grown?

My mom has lost her sister
Her husband has lost a wife
Her children have lost their mother
Her mom has lost a daughter

Sister, wife, mother, daughter
Cigarettes always causing a slaughter
Lung, then brain cancer ravaged her body
Remember these words each and everybody

How many more lives have got to be lost?
The addiction of nicotine at any cost.
When will it be over, when will it end?
Love and grief is all that's left for us to send

Memories in the past, gone and forgotten
Feelings of anger and sorrow have begotten
From this untimely death, that didn't have to occur
Now her life has become just a blur

What I still can't believe is my mom
and my aunt's husband Chris
Still smoking even though they will miss
A sister and wife, yet still will not admit
That this fate can happen to either one of them

How strong and blinding is this addiction
Right in front of them, but still no reflection
Of what can happen to either one of them
But neither one really gives a damn
About who will miss them if this happens to them
Still oblivious and into their own blind eyes
No matter how much or loud my cries
Warnings on packages and also my lips
But the only reactions from them are short mindless snips

Like: We all have to die sometime

Or: Everything causes cancer, time after time

MY IN LAWS

My In- Laws are the best, anyone could ever wish for.
They are always there, to watch our kids,
    whenever we walk out the door.
No matter, where we need to go,
    they never do complain,
and are always willing, to lend a hand,
    when we cannot maintain.

My In-Laws are the best, anyone can see.
If I didn't know any better,
    I'd think they loved my kids more than me.
Always willing to give, everything they've got;
you can only imagine,
    how spoiled my kids have got.

What would we do, without the In-Laws in my life?
Thank God for the parents,
    of my beautiful little wife.
Without them in our life, who knows what we'd do?
Herding our children off to daycare,
    like they were animals in the zoo?

Not to mention the money,
    that my wife and I have saved.
Who knows when we will ever,
    be able to repay,
for their love and kindness, towards the kids and us?
They always give all their love,
    without an ounce of fuss.

**My In-Laws are the best, the world has ever seen.
Always they are loving,**
 never are they mean.
So, if you ever ask me,
 who are the best In-Laws you will ever see?
I'll have to tell you mine,
 George and Francis the best In-Laws for eternity.

GENERATIONS

Sisters and brothers,
    fathers and mothers.
The tapestry of life,
    a husband and his wife.

Generations to come,
    a little love for some.
Passing on a family name,
    life is but just a game.

Where are we going?
Where have we been?
No time left to sing.
If? Why? Where? And when?

Offspring passing on heredity,
    sometimes for eternity.
Sometimes it gets cut really short,
    when thoughts of children they abort.

Generations, one right after the other,
    some have a sister; others have a brother.
Some don't have any to pass along,
    then it's the end, of their lovely song.

MOTHERHOOD

Motherhood or fatherhood, which one is best?
In my opinion, motherhood has got to pass the test
Sometimes I think there is no comparison
When it comes to love for daughters and sons

Mothers are the best; maybe it's just natural
Or maybe all men are just full of bull
Mothers have patience, and love that is so true
While fathers have missed chances
     that they always blew

Mothers' kindness and security always go too far
They buy the kids everything from clothing to a car
Mothers never think twice
     when it comes to the love, they share
With fathers sometimes,
     you can't tell how much they care

Mothers' love always goes beyond the call of duty
They always give in to their children,
     even when they're moody
Men on the other hand always lose their temper
Something they wish they could control
For the love always gets hampered

Mothers love lasts for eternity
Even after the children are gone, dead and buried
In their mothers' eye, children can do nothing wrong
Because their love for them is just too strong

GRANDMOTHERS

Grandmothers give you a reason to live,
a reason to love, a reason to give,
a reason to go on, with your life,
no matter how hard you deal with the strife.

Grandmothers are your link to the past,
your link to the future, no matter how fast,
it goes by, you cannot forget,
about your history, please don't let,
your life pass on by without thanking them.
Show the love you have for them.

Grandmothers are the best, no matter which one.
Whether from your father or mother,
they are still number one,
they won't last forever, soon they will be gone.
Cherish all the moments and visit very often.

Grandmothers make the world go around,
they pick you up, when you're feeling down.
Just think about them, when you need to smile,
even if you're on the road driving mile after mile,
or whether you're at home all alone,
or sitting and talking on the telephone.
Remember them till their very last day,
after the funeral and past eternity's play.
In your mind, their memory will forever stay.

A STAY AT HOME MOM

A stay at home mom is what every woman wants to be
If it is not, it is what God wants them to be
Maybe it's just what I've heard,
    but it makes sense to me
It would be nice if my wife could stay home
    with our family
Instead of struggling and worrying about all the bills
She could be at home having all of the thrills
Of watching our children grow up in front of her eyes
Instead of coming home from work every day
    to a brand-new surprise

A stay at home mom and raising their own
    children and family
Is what every woman should strive to be
Instead of becoming a career woman
    and making all of the money
They could be at home serving up
    all the milk and honey
To their children and their husbands
    who have been at work
Putting up with the bosses who always are a jerk
Nurturing and loving all the children around
Instead of being at work themselves,
    working their fingers to the ground

A stay at home mom is what my wife wants to be
She tells me every day, how much she thinks I'm lazy
Now that I've lost my job and don't want another
She says I'm a deadbeat dad and I am such a bother

She says she doesn't care that I'm now going to school
She just thinks I'm lazy and trying to be cool
If we could have it any other way
God only knows, I'm trying the best every day
To find a solution that would cure both of our ills
She could be at home every day
      instead of looking at picture stills

I wish we could have it any other way
I can't help that I'm an entrepreneur
      and I am dreaming every day
Of a different solution than me getting a new job
That doesn't mean I'm nothing but a big fat slob
Please have patience and don't give up on me
Your dreams will come true one day
      just you wait and see

LITTLE JOYS IN MY LIFE

Little joys in my life,
    include not arguing, with my little wife.
Spending time with my children,
    trying to avoid yelling again and again.

Watching TV, spending so much time,
listening to the radio, another rappers rhyme.
Being able to write a poem, maybe a new song.
Working out at the gym,
    everyday getting a little bit more strong.

Sitting on the computer, learning new information.
There's so much to do in this great wonderful nation.
Entering all the contests and all of the sweepstakes.
Eating at fancy restaurants,
    juicy lobsters and thick steaks.

Playing volleyball, tennis, baseball, and bowling.
Reading magazines, books, email, just scrolling.
So much information, so little time.
Always in a hurry, to use just one more rhyme.

Going to the movies, watching anything new.
If only I had the time, that's what I would do.
Dreaming of the Oscars,
    wishing I were on their stages.
Receiving my awards,
    daydreaming through life's pages.

FAMILY

Aaron is my firstborn,
born to me and my wife.
Sometimes he brings on a lot of scorn,
Anger, happiness and a little strife.

Joshua is the middle child,
the son that looks like me.
Sometimes he can be pretty wild,
He's such a sight to see.

Kirsten is our baby girl,
barely fifteen months old.
She's the most beautiful pearl,
even more precious than gold.

Then there's me and Debbie my wife,
together for half of our lives.
Together for the rest of our life,
the love between us thrives.

So here you have my family.
Aaron, Joshua, Kirsten and Debby.
A lot of love, a lot to see,
starting our loving family tree.

AARON

My baby first born Aaron,
      ---I can remember when he was born.
It seems just like yesterday,
      ---all my emotions they were torn.
My whole life changed,
      ---in one split second.
I remember never wanting children,
      ---then the feeling began to end.
Day after day,
      ---as Aaron began to grow.
I thank God above,
      ---for what he was trying to show.
That children are a blessing, and a responsibility,
      ---not just a result of sex and promiscuity.
I can't even imagine having an abortion.
Why do they get pregnant?
When it's so easy to use protection.
As of today,
      ---Aaron is already eight.
Most of the time he's a spoiled brat,
      ---but sometimes he's really great.
I know it won't be long,
      ---until he's out the door.
I wish he only knew,
      ---what life had in store.
I hope he doesn't make,
      ---the same mistakes as me.
The sky is the limit,
      ---he can become anything he wants to be.

JOSHUA

Joshua is our middle child--white as can be
He is the one son-- that looks the most like me
He has a birthmark-- on the side of his chest
The teacher from his school-- says he's one of her best
Joshua can be a brat --just like his big brother Aaron
When they get to playing-- they forget about sharing
They are always fighting-- yelling and screaming
Then he comes running
    --with tears that are all streaming
So far, he is the loudest-- of our three children
You can't even imagine-- how tough it has been
For me to control
    -- my temper, my anger and my patience
Sometimes I need to spend
    -- some more time all alone in silence
Joshua my middle child-- is a lot like me
Sometimes it is so surprising-- I wonder how it can be
So much heredity-- that you pass on to your children
You never know which traits
    -- that you are going to send
Sometimes you send good-- other times they are bad
Sometimes they make you happy
    -- other times they make you sad
Sometimes you don't notice them
    --sometimes you can't help it
Sometimes you don't want to
    -- admit the traits that came from you

KIRSTEN

Kirsten is our third child---pretty as can be
The prettiest most gorgeous girl
      ---whom you will ever see
I can't believe God's blessed us
      ---with three beautiful children
I can't believe what a blessing
      ---these three children have been
Kids are so funny---and so unpredictable
Kirsten amazes us with her antics
      ---each and every day
She is so cute—so pretty—and so adorable
She makes us laugh so hard
      ---whenever she starts to play
Kirsten is our gift from God---such a beautiful sight
When I think of the future
      ---I get overcome with fright
Knowing what the future---will soon have in store
When she becomes a teenager
      ---and boyfriends are knocking on the door
I know right now she is only—sixteen months old
But time flies by so fast
      ---these thoughts make me so cold
Soon she will get married
      ---and walking down the aisle
And all the childhood memories
      ---will become just a pile
Of photographs in a photo album
      —that stretches over a mile
And anytime I think of her
      ---it will bring to my face a smile

FISHING AT SALTON SEA

I used to fish at the Salton Sea
With my stepdad and brother
You can only imagine the degrees
From the suns heat that always smothered

Sometimes the fish would bite
Other days were all just wasted
Days sometimes ended in a fight
Then our skin became all basted

Scaling and gutting fish
Is not such a pretty sight
If I had just one wish
It would be to never fight

With my stepdad or brother
Or my friends so few there were
Or my hard-working mother
Whose love for us was so pure

THE LIBRARY

Terry, Tim, Sandra, Donna and Joyce
Every single day I would just try to voice
My opinions for improvements
      and all my common sense
Every single day, you can't imagine how tense
It got when no one would listen to me
I thought we lived in a country
Where we all were forever free
To speak our mind and voice our opinions
But apparently not there
Where they all tried to control the dominion
All of them with degrees
      they thought they were so smart
Put their degrees together worthless like a stinky fart
Tim with his big words trying to sound like a genius
My small simple vocabulary,
      I think is much more precious
Terry was so old she should've retired a long time ago
I'm not trying to be mean,
      but you can only imagine how slow
She was when checking out the books
      and even more so
When answering questions on the telephone
Don't get me started with Sandra
She was a nice person and all
But when it came down to common sense,
      she had none at all
Mind you this is just my opinion,
      you don't have to agree
But isn't it great to live in the USA,
      where my speech is forever free?

Joyce was unique in her own special way
She rode the bus from Palm Springs to Indio
    every single day
She didn't have a car; I don't know if she could drive
I cannot imagine being carless, how do you survive?
She looked somewhat manly
    with her short hair and her walk
Start a conversation, for hours that woman could talk
Talked for nearly an hour,
    every single day before we opened up
But never once did Donna, ever tell her to shut up
But if I was just five to ten minutes late
The sh*t would hit the fan,
    and Donna would become irate
I told her I would stay over, and make up all the time
She told me to shut up, you can't do that,
    and just be on time
So many rules and regulations,
    I think a few Donna tried to make up
From the first day that she started
No shorts, no gum, and her favorite was shut up
Shorts and tee shirts without buttons
In her opinion was unprofessional
But when you let stinky vagrants in
I don't see any need to be professional
Call me a rebel, call me what you will
All the anger and resentment, is with me to this day still
Maybe one day I'll be able to forget about all the pain
Until that day arrives, I'll do the best to try to maintain
I'll write another poem about my job, which was so insane
I can't help my life, always seems to go against the grain

CALLING CENTER BLUES

Working at a call center is what I now do
Answering phones all day long, it feels like a zoo
Every different customer
      is a different animal in their own right
Sometimes they yell and make you feel like getting into a fight

Answering the phone,
      from the morning till the middle of the night
Putting up with their irate-ness
      gives my brain such a fright
Arguing about their orders, services and their bills
Sometimes it gets so bad;
      you want to start popping pills

Phone call after phone call, you do what you can
Another hour goes by;
      your brain feels like a human trash can
There's only so much you can do,
      for the customer to pacify
Their anger and unhappiness,
      sometimes we can never satisfy

Equipment is not working; their bill is way too high
Every single call a new adventure
      makes you want to cry
Hearing very sad sob stories,
      you try to be nice to them all
Sometimes the customer yells so much,
      it makes you feel oh so small

Rules and regulations keep you
>from helping all of them
Sometimes you will get lucky
>and finally answer a real gem
That one rare customer that's so nice
>it makes you feel so great
They almost make you forget
>about the customers that are so irate

When you get home at night,
>no one really understands your point of view
Then that makes you mad some more,
>your spouse becomes a customer too
You try to separate your work life
>from your home life,
nothing really helps
So, the next day comes again and you swim through it
just like Michael Phelps

THE MENTALLY ILL

The mentally ill are depressed and can get really sad
Sometimes they get really loud, angry and then mad

Most of the times they just can't help it
They get out of control and just can't stop it

Uncontrollable, it's real sad to see
They're so much more alike than you and me

Some brains are fried, and some are addicted
So hard they try to break free,
      and still others are afflicted

Almost all of them smoke
It's such a shame to see
I will never smoke
It's such a waste of money

Spending all day smoking or watching TV
There's so much more to life for them to see

What's the use for the drugs to make them better?
If all they do is smoke and eventually get cancer
There is so much more to life, it is so sad to see
Wasting their life on nicotine and drinking up coffee

Most could keep jobs if they just tried
Even the worst cases with the brains all fried
I treat them all the same, I try not to judge
I treat them like friends, not like a pile of sludge

SPENDAHOLIC

What I am is a Spendaholic.
It is worse than being an alcoholic.
If you were one, you would know it was true.
These words I tell you make me so blue.

I wish I could stop, but it's just too hard.
Every single penny gets spent like a card,
you deal in a card game, play after play.
I just wish there was some other way.

I know I have bills, but I just don't care.
All I want to do with my money is share,
and spend without a single thought,
and not worry about what I ought,
to do or what I ought to pay.
I know you tell me every day.

I don't listen or maybe I can't,
maybe I'm sick with a spending slant.
Something I wish I could avoid,
but all I ever do is just get annoyed,
with myself and then I spend some more,
every single moment I walk outside the door.

THE OTHER DAY

The other day I received a rejection letter,
telling me my poems are doggerel and cliché.
Next time I write, I'll try to make them a little better,
but I don't know if I can,
      because I always write that way.
Most of the time I just get form letters
    with little or no reply,
but every once in a while,
    I get some comments that tell me why,
they didn't choose them to add to their magazine,
and I really appreciate them,
    whether long or really lean.
Sometimes when I start to write,
I don't know what will come out next,
but then it becomes a beautiful sight.
Maybe I am under a curse or a hex.
 I appreciate everyone's comments,
whether they like them, or they do not.
These poems to me are like cement,
that you pour into a page
    like a brand-new parking lot.
Who knows if I will ever stop,
these jewels that come right out.
My life is now an open book that will pop,
when you turn the pages of my brains open spout.
Another day just passed on by,
wrote a few more pages.
No end to these poems that I try,
to tell stories of my life's endless stages.

JOY

Have you ever felt,
true joy and happiness?
I have only felt,
true feelings of loneliness.

Joy is what I need.
Where is it to be found?
Am I full of greed?
Can the feeling ever be unbound?

Joy is what you have.
Joy is what I want.
I wish I knew how to save,
so, the desire would stop the haunt.

Joy is all around,
If I only knew,
I wish it would surround,
like the sky's wide-open blue.

I did find joy in writing.
This little rhyme for you.
I hope it was kind of exciting,
Not knowing what I was going to do.

PROLIFIC

P eople keep telling me I am prolific,
    I just say OK

R eality is I am just so damn depressed
    and have no other outlet or way

O ther than that I just love to write
    so here is another poem to say

L ive life to the fullest,
    you never know when it will be your very last day

I sn't this much better than going postal,
    I know I must pray

F or patience and tolerance of stupidity
    from people I see along life's highways or bay

I nsulting my intelligence
    with words only found in a dictionary

C larity in thought,
    not confusion making my mind go astray

MY OBSESSION

Poems are my obsession,
One hundred percent
my own possession.
These words I know,
will forever stay,
On this planet,
there is just no other way,
For me to rationalize and voice,
My words and questions;
I have no other choice,
To spread throughout the land.
These words,
which sometimes are quite grand,
Can put a smile on your face.
And all your worries
you will never trace,
As long as you read and try not to wander,
Too fast through the page
or else you will squander,
The thoughts that at the time I had to write,
About my life,
whether about happy times or about the blight.

WHY THE RHYME

So, you don't like rhymes
I think that's a crime
You call them forced
I say but of course

Any excuse will do
When it comes to
Creativity
and simplicity

Forced or doggerel
Simple or for real
These are my thoughts
Enjoy or take your shots

Critics and critiques
Mystery and mystiques
Small words of reflection
Each going in the same direction

Depression, love, suicide or hate
Each one of these can be bad or great
Depending on eyes of the beholder
Some are so hot, others are much colder

Change one word and it is not the same
Rhymes in my poems are not a game
I love to rhyme and always will
Like a drug addict, the rhyme is my pill

WAR OF WORDS

You don't want a war with me
Because you will never win
When it comes to rhymes you see
I'll take you places you've never been
Simple is what I am, take it or leave it
But don't complain or try to change
Cause, then I feel so crappy and then I want to split
Please just enjoy my limited word range
I write what I feel and try to rhyme
Cause to me it flows much smoother
Then prose or free verse time after time
Don't make me feel like a loser
Simplicity is who I am; it could be my middle name
I try real hard not to appear over intellectual
Cause it makes life too much of a game
We should all just be happy with words big or small
I don't count the syllables, I just don't care
I just write until I am through with the thought
Sometimes short or long, until I reach a final stare
Inside my brain until a feeling is caught
I rewrite inside my head before it comes out on screen
Thank God for computers,
I can always highlight and delete
Before printing the poem out on paper for the entire
world to be seen
And read in spare time whether standing
    or having a seat
Instead of criticism, there should be more praise
For what is good throughout words we share
So, think next time you sit, read and gaze
And read words that were written with care

CREATIVITY

Creativity borders on insanity
Leaves falling from the tree

Insanity disguised by creativity
No one knows what is to be

Writing after reading, hoping not to steal
Words or phrases bringing out the zeal

Sleep deprivation ends with a rush
Of ideas onto the paper, like a painter's brush

Stress or strain causing unknown energy
Channeled into words of splendor and beauty

Colors, images, thoughts of the past
Transferred into poems that will forever last

RELEASE

I'll try to describe the release I get when I write
It's almost like freeing your mind,
    just like flying a kite
Free your mind, your spirit and your soul
Let the words flow, lose all of control

Don't try to think too hard
Or the words might just get marred
Relax, stay calm and then concentrate
Another poem will come out and it will sound so great

Sometimes they go in such diverse directions
Every single line can describe different reflections
Of life's journeys and travels in the past
Then I don't know which line to make last

So, I sit and think and write
    another paragraph or two
Of my life, my sights,
    my hobbies and what I like to do
I try not to bore
Sometimes it is a chore
There is so much more
Of words I have in store

I hope I spread some joy, a little bit of happiness
If nothing else, I've released a little bit of stress

A MILLION THINGS

A million or two things, running through my mind.
What I need to do and trying to be kind.
All at the same moment, I don't know what to do.
So, I'll just sit down and write a poem or two.

Millions of ideas and emotions running through
My mind, body, and spirit, what should I do?
Prioritize and number and set a few new goals.
Maybe then I could accomplish all of my goals.

So much information I cannot control.
All of the emotions starting to take their toll.
On every part of my body, my mind, and my spirit.
All of these feelings, they just won't let
Me concentrate on what needs to be done.
I don't even have time, to have a little fun

All I want to do is have some peace and quiet.
A little tranquility I wish that I could buy it.
If I can't, I might just go berserk.
Then once again I'll start acting like a jerk.

MEMORIES

Here I sit, as I turn the page
Of life, another book unto the stage
I perform, read, speak, sleep and eat
How do I keep up and stay on my feet?

I want to give in, give up and quit
Too much to do, so all I do is sit
Thinking, wondering, words running through
My unstable mind, then time just flew

Another hour flies by, what have I done?
Another page with no remembrance is gone
I try to recall what I have just read
But with no memory, I wish I were dead

Life is a movie; we each have our parts to play
Some move on so easily, some dread another day
School, families, careers then death
Flashing memories until our last breath

CONVOLUTED

Convoluted is what you say
Premeditated and I like it that way
Never to change, always the same
Waiting to face life's prolonged game

Convoluted, with scrambled thoughts anew
Everything sticks to something else just like glue
Nothing starts with the here and now
One thing leads to another until you get plowed

Convoluted again and again
Long winded, some say I have been
Drawn out language not hard to understand
Elaborate story needed to be told un-bland

Convoluted, but I don't think so
It is not my fault the way my life will go
There is always a cause before the effect
So, I will continue to tell my story direct

Convoluted if you will, but I don't buy it
Difficult sometimes to understand all of it
Complicated maybe, but hey so what's new
Convoluted should be my middle name,
     so true so true

THE DAY SLIPPED AWAY

Another day--- just slipped away
Into the past--- went by too fast
Where did it go--- I was too slow
To do everything that needed to be done
I'll put it off until tomorrow
Try to contain all my sorrow
Forget about what could've been
Forget about if and when
I do the things that need to be
Instead I sit in front of the T.V.
Wasting my life,
Listening to my wife
Complain about all the bills
Life should be full of way more thrills
If only we had a few more dollars
Each of us would use less hollers
At each other using profanity
Won't someone please stop this insanity?
Before it's too late and we both give up
On this marriage and decide to quit
At least we'd stop telling each other to shut up
If I had the nerve to take my wrist and slit
But I don't, so I won't
So, I'll just put up with it
And try to live another day
The best I can in peace and harmony

THE OTHER DAY
I STOPPED

The other day I stopped
To notice the colors of the leaves
Then all around I looked
and saw the effects of the breeze

I looked up to the sky
In its beautiful different blues
Every moment and direction I try
To appreciate the immense amount of hues

I admired the diversity
Of mountains in the distance
So big, powerful, and mighty
With just one momentary glance

So much all around
to admire all of God's creation
from the sky to the ground
no matter which country or which nation

ALWAYS LATE

Always late, no matter how hard I try.
I'll probably be late, for my funeral,
    the day after I die.

Always late, never seem to be on time.
I'd probably be late, if I was committing a crime.

Always late, just don't understand.
I'd probably be late, if I was a musician in a band.

Always late, I don't know why.
I'd probably be late, if I was a pilot and had to fly.

Always late, I try really hard,
to be on time, but it's just too hard.

Always late, it seems so crazy.
I guess my excuse is, I'm just too lazy.
I even set all my clocks ahead,
    but it just doesn't work.
Then I'm late again, and I start feeling like a jerk.
Never on time; story of my life.
I bet I was late, to the marriage to my wife
Always late, no matter how fast I drive.
I guess I'll be late, forever, as long as I'm alive.

ALWAYS CRITICAL

You are always critical
      Never do you support me
Stop being so analytical
      Instead you should open your eyes and see
Why are you so mean?
      Seldom are you kind
Feelings are so lean
      Your thoughts you need to unwind
When I want you here,
      You are always over there
When I shed a tear,
      I look around, and you are nowhere
Whenever you are happy
      I am always sad
And when I'm feeling crappy
      Then you are so glad
Whenever I am up and in a good mood
      You bring me down and fill me with sadness
Always the opposite of my mood
      Whenever I get mad,
      you seem to gleam with gladness
Whenever I am cold--- You are always hot
When I start to scold--- You decide I should not
Is there no in between--- Loving feelings and hatred
So much more than happy and mean
      In this life before it is wasted
Happy, sad, love, and a little bit of hate
      Hot, cold, warm, never
Wouldn't it be nice if it were great?
      Between us forever!

ANOTHER POEM ABOUT T.V.

I'll write another poem about my love for T.V.
It's always been such a big part of my life
    including I Love Lucy
So many memories clogging up my brain
From American Bandstand, MTV, and Soul Train
I can remember Night Gallery
Outer Limits and Dynasty
Whether it's scary or even about money
Or whether it's funny like three's company
Or serious like Dragnet, Adam 12, or Emergency
Old shows like Bonanza and
    Little House on The Prairie
Will always be classics for future generations to see
I know I'll forget a few
Like little shows nobody ever knew
Children's programs on Saturday mornings
    like Ark Two
Sigmund And the Sea Monsters
 and The Land Before Time
Scooby Doo, The Flintstones,
    The Jetsons and Run Joe Run
So many memories are waiting for recall
Some were pretty big, but most were really small
It's easy to remember some,
    but hard to remember them all
Every single year, adding new storage space
    to my brain's mall
Every single day always something new
I know everyone thinks my life I just blew
Watching too much TV, it will be the death of me
But what a way to go sitting in front of my T.V.

ANOTHER VACATION

Another vacation comes only once a year
All of the planning can cause many a tear
Lack of money can fill you full of fear
Sometimes it is too much; your mind you cannot clear

Planning and preparation sometimes it's too much
Overwhelming feelings they have become such
A headache for you and also for me
Why does it year after year like this have to be?

Such a hassle and so much work
Running out of time then acting like a jerk
Where should we go, how long should we stay
If we had more money a hotel on the bay

Have to cut it short, and go back home
Ran out of funds, I feel so all alone
Found another bank, and a little bit more money
I guess we'll all stay longer my kids, me,
      and DEB my little honey

Find a cheap hotel, save a little cash
Try to calm down and try not to act so rash
It was a nice journey, as long as it did last
But now it is over, it went by oh so fast
Back to reality, back to the old grind
Back to overwhelming bills, that always seem to bind

ANOTHER DAY INTO THE FUTURE

Another day passing,
    into the future.
Never to return,
    forever it is gone.

Looking back and forward,
    not knowing what to do.
Trying not to be too bored,
    finding new things to do.
Always needing money,
    paying all the bills.
Next month need more money,
    to pay even more bills.

Living just above broke,
    living just above poverty.
I heard you just spoke,
    I don't want your pity.

To be financially free,
    and independently wealthy.
It's the life for me,
    definitely for me.

How do I get there
    knowing where I've been?
Anywhere but here,
    then I know I'll win.

ANOTHER BASEBALL GAME

I watched my son play baseball today.
It was so exciting---I must say.
So close a game, they almost won.
If nothing else, I hope they had fun.
They almost won---it was so close.
Too many mistakes---nobody rose,
to the occasion of MVP.
It was a toss-up, between about two or three.
Down to the last inning,
got really exciting.
Five more runs and we would be winning.
Down to the end, it was really nail biting.
We are at bat, scored only four and tied.
The important thing is, at least they tried.
Too many coaches, telling them what to do;
they get so confused and don't know what to do.
They try to teach them, to run through first base,
but too often they slow down, and their hit is a waste.
They get thrown out, because they slow down.
Then their smile turns into a frown.
If they would listen, run fast as they could,
they'd all be safe at first, the way they always should.
At least they're learning and trying really hard.
Year after year, moving up the game card.
Another year, another season,
I hope their playing, for all the right reasons.

ANOTHER DAY ANOTHER FIGHT

Another day, another fight.
You'd think by now,
we would get it right.

Another day, for no reason at all,
fighting and fussing. I'd rather be at the mall.

Another day, what did I do?
Another fight, we just blew.

Another fight, not again.
Too much pain, that's all its ever been.

Another fight, another day.
I just wish; there was some other way.

Instead of fighting, we should be kissing.
Just think of all the love, we have been missing.

No more fights, no more days,
wasted arguing, it just doesn't pay.

It's not worth the pain,
and all the stress and strain.
Another fight just might drive me insane.
I know if we try hard, we both can maintain.

ANOTHER DAY FUTURE'S GONE

Another day is passing
Future's been and gone
Thoughts are ever lasting
Sing another song

Passing the day away
Wondering what to do
Should I go or should I stay
So much there is to do

Another passing moment
Another shifting thought
Another second well spent,
in deep meaning thought

Another glimpse of time
Neither reason nor rhyme
Another grain of sand
Time was in your hand

Minutes and hours passing by
What have you done?
Trying to just squeeze by,
hoping that you're done

ANOTHER FIGHT

Another fight, another day.
I get so angry, I wish there was some other way,
to help me focus and learn some control,
so I won't blow up and lose all of control.

Driving home from school, I'm always in a hurry.
I can't slow down; my life is way too blurry.
I just want to relax and get home so fast.
I know the day, is not going to last.

I want some peace and quiet, when I do get home.
It never seems to happen, and then I feel so all-alone.
I want to run away but have no place to go.
So my nerves start to rattle,
and my mind begins to blow.

I lose my temper and start to yell.
Then my wife tells me, to go to hell.
I try really hard, but nothing works,
then we both become, really big jerks.

Maybe someday, I'll learn to relax,
then we can stop, all of the attacks.
Yelling and screaming, at each other,
having no money, is such a bother.

If we had more, I know it would be different.
So many happy times, we could have spent,
if we weren't so poor, and had so many bills;
life would be so full, of unlimited thrills.

ANOTHER BEAUTIFUL DAY

Another beautiful day, living in paradise.
The earth is a giant pie and we each have a slice.
To do with what we will.
Swallow it up just like a pill.

Trying to be best, never to be last.
Hoping to one day, forget about the past.
Of all the pain and memories.
Blowing in my mind, like leaves in the trees.

Forever locked in the deep canyons of my mind.
I can't believe so many people have been so kind.
Not to judge or betray my trust.
Only to love, with kind words without the lust.

Forever the earth will be full of love.
As long as GOD sends it all from up above.
And we accept and overcome our weakness.
Then we can start to overpower all the bleakness.
That seems to be rampant on this land.
But I know one day this life can be quite grand.
For you and me and all mankind.
I just can't wait for this world to unwind.
I hope you feel the same way as me.
Open your eyes and we will all be able to see.
The love of GOD radiates on all of us.
It won't be long if we avoid all of the fuss.
That life brings upon us day after day.
All that is left is for us to pray.

A LESSON I'VE LEARNED IN LIFE

A lesson I've learned in life,
Is don't take life for granted.
Be careful when picking a wife
There shouldn't be second chances.
Love the one you're with.
You never know what will transpire.
This is not a myth.
You definitely will perspire.

Fighting and arguing, sometimes it is so constant.
You'd rather be snuggling instead of always in want.
Life is so quick; you never know when it will end.
Stop being such a prick, gather your love and send
All of it to everyone, never holding back.
Sometimes to anyone, then you'll never lack
Love and affection give all you've got.
Soon your life will be over, your time is not a lot.
Don't get to the end and say I wish I had more.
When time is gone, there's no more in store.
Don't live in regret, there's too much to do.
If you don't change now, it will be too late to.

Live life to the fullest; don't let it slip on by.
No matter how hard it gets, you have got to try
To be your very best, until the very end.
You know you have so much to send.
Don't get discouraged; don't give up,
No matter how hard, don't ever stop.

ANOTHER LESSON I'VE LEARNED IN LIFE

Another lesson I've learned in life
Has got to be from my wife
It's to enjoy my children while I still have time
Before it's too late and I run out of time

Another lesson I've got to say
Spend time with my kids and learn how to play
Before they're too old and it's too late
They'll remember me either way mean or great

Now is the time that I must change
It's so hard; you may think it is strange
I don't know how to be a good dad
It sometimes seems I make everyone sad

I need to change before it's too late
Take my life and wipe clean the slate
Start all over hope it's not too hard
All my emotions I'll need to guard

Learn some patience stop getting so mad
Change my children's feelings from sadness to glad
I hope one day they all could be
The happiest children you ever could see

A DREAM COME TRUE

A dream come true has got to be
Becoming a millionaire from the lottery
Although the chances are quite small
If it did happen, I would feel a mile tall

I've won before, for only twenty-five grand
It wasn't much, but my life became un-bland
If only for a short while, it still was great
I spent it so fast, I just couldn't wait

Another dream come true, has got to be my wife
Since I met her, she has changed my life
We've been together so long it seems like forever
The vows we have made, no one can ever sever

Another dream come true, I've got to say
Are the three beautiful children,
     she has given me to this day
Growing up so fast, they'll soon all be old
Then they'll be out working
     and doing what they're told

Another dream come true or maybe just a nightmare
A house, a car, all the bills becoming such a scare
Better than an apartment
     eight years was enough for me
My life's pretty good now,
     how much greater could it be

TWENTY-FOUR HOURS

If I only had 24 hours to live
I don't know what I'd do,
    but I sure hope I would give
All of my time and all of my love
To all of the people I truly do love

If I only had 24 hours
I think I would stop and smell the flowers
If my life was cut really short
I think I would try some crazy new sport

I don't know, who really does
Know what they'd do in this situation
Maybe jump on a plane and buzz
To a beautiful brand-new nation

It would be nice to say we'd do this
It would be nice to say we'd do that
I know one thing we all sure would miss
Is giving our loved ones a goodbye kiss

It sounded so easy, what would you do
If you only had 24 hours to live
So many things to say, so many things to do
If you only had more love to give

So, this is the end of my tale
I hope it doesn't sound to pale
So, this is the end of my day
I don't know what else to say

DREAM VACATION

My dream vacation, what would it be?
I would fly to an island with plenty of trees.
Relax and enjoy and try to forget,
about all of the rushing and all of the fret.

Try to relax and have some fun.
Try not to worry about being too dumb.
Get away and enjoy it all.
Get back up if I fall.

Climb a mountain or even a hill.
To not have to take any kind of pill.
Enjoy the sun, the beach, and the sand,
to be with my love, hand in hand.

Not to worry about my bills,
tension and anger only kills.
Relax and enjoy doing new things,
new hobbies, and games, with no attached strings.

Peace and harmony, could only bring,
new adventures, for me to sing.
Never again to return,
all the bad memories have got to burn.

My dream vacation, what could it be?
A whole new life is waiting for me.

DREAMING

Write another letter
    Sing another song
Hope to get a little better
    Hope it doesn't take too long
Passing another day away
    Never to return
There's got to be a better way
    To get what we so yearn
Wanting this and wanting that
    Always wanting more
Never being satisfied
    When we walk out the door
Will we ever really find,
    What we really want?
Will we ever really mind,
    the thoughts that seem to haunt?
Juggling the thoughts day and night
    Hoping to one day sort
Always learning new insight
    Hoping never to abort
The dreams that seem to always take over
    Knowing one day that they will come true
I know if I have no more dreams, life will be over
    And then I'll never see the sky in any color blue
I wonder if others ever dream as big as me
    Or am I just a little insane
Knowing one day my dreams will be REALITY,
    not just a crazy thought inside my brain

MY SPECIAL PLACE

My special place is my living room

Changes from year to year

In my youth it was my bedroom

It was my place to shed a tear

As long as there was a T.V.

I didn't need anyone else around

This is how it will always be

You may question if my mind is sound

But my feelings will never change

From relaxation to exuberance

You may think it's strange

From enjoyment to intolerance

At least this place is mine

But you are welcome to share

And then you will see how it shines

Whether you sit on the couch or chair

THE LIVING ROOM

The living room is my special place
No other room can ever replace
The tranquility and joy I always get
When, in front of the T.V. I just let
My feelings and worries vanish away
Into the air, to forever stay
No more stress for me to worry about
As long as my T.V. works, no need to pout
This may sound strange, but I don't care
With the T.V. on, and me in my chair
I can relax and forget about life
Homework, my kids, and even my wife
No matter what color the four walls are
The T.V. in front of me takes me so far
In space and time, another place not here
It doesn't matter when or where

BIRTH SCHOOL WORK DEATH

Birth, school, work, death.
What happens in between these is life.
Happens to all, some slow, some fast
Happiness soon, praying misery won't last.

First, we are born.
If lucky raised by both parents.
Ridiculed and scorned,
Hopefully by neither parent.

Grow up through the years,
Through all the grades of school.
Avoiding all the tears,
Classmates treating you like a fool.

Find a job and go to work;
Job after job working with a bunch of jerks.
Never ending story, lucky to get away.
Thank GOD for answering when we pray.

Finally, we die, death part of life.
Luckily if we tried, left behind some kids and a wife.
If we were good accepted Jesus Christ,
As lord and savior of our life.
We could be up in heaven, side by side.

DEATH

Death comes to all, some fast some slow.
After we die, where do we go?

Up to heaven, or down to hell.
Who really knows? It's so hard to tell.

Who do we believe? Will we ever know?
Who knows the answers, to life's big top show?

God is looking down; he will leave it in our hands.
Satan is down below, laughing from the stands.

Please accept Jesus, before it is too late,
As lord and savior. His love is so great.

God with all his love sent his only son.
If we will believe, our life has begun.

LOOK AT GODS BEAUTY

Look towards the horizon
And tell me what you see
It won't be too surprising
As far as the eye can see

Rolling grassy hills
Or flat vegetation
It might give you some thrills
If you use your imagination

The beauty and the wonder
The colors and the hues
Many a different splendor
Colors of reds, greens, and blues

Everywhere you look
No matter which direction
Behind every cranny and nook
Behind every single reflection

God's beauty is all around
Whether in the sky or on the ground
Whether in the water or in the air
God's beauty is everywhere

ANTS

I just saw the lamppost, I never saw before
How many times have I looked at it
	while walking out the door?

The peeling bark on the tree looks so natural
Falling as it does slowly rolling like a ball

Down the trunk unto the ground
Next to the ants that move round and around

Coming and going, the ants never stop
You'd think they'd get tired
	and their hearts would pop

All this work with no paycheck in sight
Do they take a vacation in the middle of the night?

Are they all sleeping the same time as us?
Then they wake up to face the same old fuss

Ants and humans really aren't that different
Coming and going so fast before life is spent

THE LAWN

The weekends were so short
When my stepdad woke us up
To do yard work for sport
I just hated waking up

Pulling clover in grass
I still don't understand it
Yard work I would pass
Because I just hated it

Even to this very day
I hate mowing the lawn
One day I can only pray
That I'll never mow the lawn

Grass and weeds are such a waste
Who cares how good they look?
Yard work freedom I can taste
Memories that were a crook

THE WIND

The wind was more than just blowing
As if the sand through the air,
    looked like it was snowing
Criss-crossing through the sky,
    here and there
From horizon to horizon,
    it was everywhere

A breeze billowing to and fro
Everywhere you look, everywhere you go
Trees, with leaves scurrying through the air
Falling to the ground you can see it everywhere

Angrily blowing across the barren land
Sometimes the sights and sounds can be quite grand
You never know when it all will end
The wind has no mercy with the branches it will bend

Ferocious wind shaping the clouds in the sky
No matter how low they are, no matter how high
Coming out of nowhere,
    not knowing how long it will last
But when it does come,
    it can blow with such a blast

WAVE WATCHING

Sitting, watching the waves roll on in
Thinking about jobs, and how bad they have been
Wasting our life for a measly weekly check
Instead of enjoying life and saying what the heck

Laying on the towel, on the sandy beaches of time
Reflecting back on life, and thinking what a crime
Working for another, for hours day after day
And thinking to myself, there's gotta be a better way

A convention here, a reflection there
A glimpse of the future, becomes a blurry stare
Spur of the moment or a yearlong plan
As far as the eye can see, nothing but ocean and sand

Thinking of days gone by
And what might have been
I sit, wonder, think, and sigh
What if this, that, and what could've happened?

PEACE

Peace, love and happiness
Are all things I truly miss
Peace, love and harmony,
Sure would be nice if they could be

All together inside of me
Filling me up and voiding out the misery

Peace, joy, love in me
Could it truly ever be?
Don't mess around, tell me the truth
I here there's good stuff in the book of Ruth
I guess I should read it, I here its real swell
I know I don't want to end up in hell

Peace, love, and tenderness too
Have all these feelings happened to you

Love, joy, freedom and peace
Maybe one day I'll receive a new lease
On life, on love, on happiness too
Maybe one day I'll feel just like you

PEACE, LOVE AND HAPPINESS

Peace, love and happiness
These three things are what I miss
When will the world be as one?
Feel the power of the moon and sun

Read a word then write it down so forever
You'll keep alive feelings so whenever
You are lonely, depressed or unhappy
The words can shine through no matter how sappy

It's never too late to change the world we live in
Turn towards the light and turn your back on sin
One by one we can all change this planet
Don't give in to despair so don't ever let

Feelings of anger, rage or emotion
Cloud your vision for world peace and love
Calm your worries like waves on the ocean
Peace on earth,
     attainable with a little help from above

Poetry means different things to different people
Words shine through while other times they just blur
Some are dull, unfocused and flat,
     others sharp like a steeple
However they move you, don't take it for granted,
just let them stir
Inside your brain, ready to recall
They'll pick you up if you ever fall

DESTINY

Who knows what your destiny holds?
In the future when your past unfolds
Memories, happy or sad, from the past
Mold your life, but how long will they last

Your destiny is in your own two hands
Take it by the reigns;
        don't view it from the grandstands
Anything is possible; we all have the same start
The final destination is where we all will depart

Decisions will mold and determine your life
Marriage, children a husband or wife
Houses, cars, travel, hobbies and friends
Mistakes, apologies all making amends

Don't dwell on the past but instead on possibility
Focus on strengths not on improbabilities
Whatever you can dream you can achieve
All it takes is for you to believe

From past to future, from hate to love
We cannot control what comes from above
No one knows what or why things happen
The future can make all of the past simply flatten

Dream big, not small cause everything is possible
All you have to do is try, make failure impossible
The only true failure is not trying at all
Future possibilities are anything but small

The sky is the limit, dream big as you can
Try with all of your might,
    like you just don't give a damn
Shoot for the stars and you will reach the moon
Don't limit your goals and you will achieve them soon

Take this message and take it to heart
No need to wait, you only need to start
Conceive, believe and soon you will achieve
Don't put it off, just need to believe

IT AINT OVER

It ain't over until you die
Don't give up until you try
Don't be too ashamed to cry
Spread your wings, like an eagle, you can fly
The end of one chapter is just the beginning
Losing is over its time to start winning
Think happy thoughts and then you'll be grinning
The past is over, forget about past sinning

The future is now, take hold with both hands
Soon you'll be watching from life's grandstands
The bleachers of life and all its demands
Are left in the dust
       and now life beckons your commands

There is no limit to what life has in store
Turn another corner and open another door
Turn the page of life; don't let it become a chore
Spread your wings, like an eagle,
       and then you will soar

A stranger from nowhere comes into your life
You think about your future, family and wife
Could this be the beginning of a brand-new life?
Is this a dream come true being sliced with a knife?
With precision and accuracy like nothing before
Never imagined while walking out the front door
Could this be reality, all your dreams are in store
God's intervention with prayers answered galore

THE INTERNET

The computer and the Internet,
are such great tools for everyone.
They can help you in so many ways,
    that you will never let,
another day pass by without having a little fun.

Not so many years ago the Internet was just a dream,
now it has become, almost too mainstream.
I don't know anyone that doesn't have a computer.
I guess they are out there,
    but they've got to have the stir,
of emotions and feelings of wanting one;
if not for themselves,
    then maybe for their daughter or son.

The Internet might seem to be too intimidating,
but once you learn and start to surf along.
You will want to sing,
I know it won't be too long.

The Internet is simple if you will only try,
I hope you look up some information
    long before you die.
Don't be afraid just jump into it,
then you will find there is nothing to it.

The Internet is waiting; what are you waiting for?
Get up off your butt and get out of the door.
Find yourself a computer and have yourself some fun.
Don't wait another minute it's there for everyone.

ARMED FORCES

The army, the air force, the marines and navy
All these armed forces just waiting for me
I admire and look up to anyone who could join
But personally, for me I don't think I could join

Being told what to do, 24 hours a day
That's no life for me, no matter what the pay
I respect and admire the people that can
Put up with the BS, the bureaucracy and the man

Not for me, it wasn't my calling
But if they ever needed me, or if they were falling
I would be there to support in any other way
Hand in hand or if they just needed to pray

The navy, the ships, the oceans all around
I'd be afraid it would sink and then I would drown
The air force would be nice; I sure would love to fly
But then there's the chance of the plane
     falling out of the sky

The marines I've heard are
     the first one's on the scene
I here they're the biggest,
     the baddest, and are pretty mean
The army is the last of these four
They'll always be in a need for just a few more

FOOD

Body tired, energy worn thin.
Brain tired from the mind within.

Arms aching from my shoulders on down
Couldn't even support a royal kings crown
Holding up the head and all of its weight
The pain I cannot bear, it is much too great

Legs aching from the toes on up
Feel like lying down all day and never standing up

Whole body aching from neck down to the waist
How did my life become such a waste?
Entire body aching inside and out
The pain always makes me want to scream and shout

How did my body get over come with this affliction?
Overeating disorder ---food always the addiction
No matter how much I eat I always want some more
I always get hungry once I walk outside the door

A love affair with food
The sight puts me in the mood
I can never get enough
Food is such great stuff

THREE SISTERS

If I had three sisters what would it be like?
Wouldn't it be funny to watch them ride a bike?
To scrape their knees when they fell.
And listening to them scream and yell.

It would also be funny to see,
All of their dates climbing a tree,
After our dad chased them away.
Having three sisters would be too hard for me.

I can only imagine the fights we would have.
All of the memories both happy and sad.
Imagining this just makes me crazy.
I could stop now if I was a bit more lazy.

I'll keep going and write a few lines more.
I'll try not to overcome you with any bore.

I can only imagine the dresses they'd wear.
And how mad they would get
    if and when they would tear.
I know it sure would be hard to find time.
To use the bathroom,
    this stops my thoughts on a dime

I think I've used enough imagination.
To have three sisters,
    I know I would be in deep desperation.

BOUNCE

I gotta go, it's time for me to bounce

Can't stay here, there's too much for me to do
Just too busy with things I need to trounce
Like going to the bank, or taking kids to the zoo

I gotta go, it's time for me to bounce

Can't stay here, I'll see you in a while
When I come back, I'll be able to announce
All the things I got done, your face will gain a smile

I gotta go, it's time for me to bounce

Can't stay here, there's too much on my agenda
I use up all my energy, what's left is not an ounce
Of sanity in my brain, all my troubles I'd love to renounce

I gotta go, it's time for me to bounce

From one place to another, so many for me to be
I can't keep track, my mind is in a
    constant state of flounce
Moving back and forward,
    just a thin line before insanity

A CRAZY WORLD

Look around, a crazy world is what you see
Doesn't matter where you live or in what country
Everywhere you look, insanity is in the air
In everybody's eyes, you can see all of the despair

A crazy world surrounds each and every one of us
So many fights, wars, and so much fuss
Disease, famine, pain in every measure
Focus on Jesus, he is the one and only cure

When the world turns crazy
And everything is so hazy
Turn your eyes toward our savior
For Jesus's love is just so pure

Inward or outward, the crazy world affects us all
So, don't give up because your problems
    are really small
Don't let them control you, Jesus is in control
Turn your life over to Jesus,
    heaven is waiting for your soul

In the meantime, this crazy world is still a mess
Even more reason to worship Jesus
    so he can forever bless
Your life, your family and loved ones
    here on this earth
Because this crazy world is way overdue
    for a brand-new rebirth

YOU ARE SO VAIN

You are so vain
Because the world drove you insane
You never know wrong from right
And always got yourself into a fight

So vain and insecure
No difference between what is filth and what is pure
Sin and disobedience disguised as being strong
Not knowing your vanity makes everything so wrong

Vanity and insecurity lead you astray
Now you need to worship Jesus and learn how to pray
Pray for forgiveness and the reasons for your sin
Self-reflection before the new you can begin

Insecurity leads to vanity right before your eyes
Sometimes it sneaks up on you
    and becomes such a surprise
Vanity can lead to humility with just a little work
So, when you talk to others,
    you don't act like such a jerk

Confidence is OK, just don't take it so far
Because if you take it too far, vanity will always scar
Those who you love and have taken for granted
Instead of love, they will only know vanity seeds
    you have planted

THE END IS NEAR

The end is near, Jesus is on his way
I've heard these words so long and for so many days
It's hard to take it serous, but just look around
Disease, death, negativity,
    it seems like it's the only sound

You hear it on the news, you see it on T.V.
Lockdown orders, rights stripped away
    is all that I see
Jesus must be on his way,
    so much fear around the globe
Maybe there'd be more faith,
    if everyone read the book of Job

This plague could just be a wakeup call
To separate all the weak from all of the strong
It could also be a time to stand up before we all fall
And unwittingly take upon us
    the mark of the beast which is so wrong

Wake up everyone don't believe the lies
The truth is right in front of you
Wake up everyone it's time to open your eyes
We all have choices, what will you do

Following like sheep to a slaughter and die
Or come to your senses and choose Jesus
The way, the truth, and the life, why not try
To pray for forgiveness, avoid eternity in hell,
    if you simply believe and choose Jesus

THE MOON GLIDING THROUGH THE NIGHT

A Poem inspired by a suggestion from Joni Russo

The moon glides through the night....
The stars twinkle so bright
To some it gives such a delight
To others it gives a fright

The moon is big then gets really small
Over time it seems it might just fall
Out of the sky and into the ocean
That would be a crazy scene

The stars twinkle oh so bright
The ones that don't are planets you know
The scene mesmerizes and is a beautiful sight
If the sky is clear, the moon will glow

The moon and the stars gliding through
The nighttime sky just like a stew
Cooking and simmering inside a pot
The sight is mixed and then it is not

The moon glides through the sky so bright
Cutting through the twinkling stars at night
Until the sun starts creeping up along the horizon
Then all that fills the sky is a beautiful bright sun

COLORFUL CANVAS IN THE SKY

A poem Inspired from a Jeff King photo

Colorful canvas in the sky
Colors so beautiful it can make you cry
With tears of happiness that God has made
Through the palm trees that are hidden by shade

Blue, pink, orange skies behind
    scattered clouds in the sky
Fading and spreading so wonderful for our eyes
God's beauty always shines through in the desert sky
No human can invent colors
    from the fingers of God if they tried

The Coachella valley has palm trees
    with skies of colorful beauty
That change throughout the day
    from dawn to dusk for all to see
Don't blink your eyes, unless you want
    to miss another scene
From God's canvas that comes alive
    with inspiration like a fine cuisine

From the bluest of blues,
    to the entire pallet from yellow to red
Purple and violet fading into one another
    and darkening into night
Squeezing out the lightest of yellow,
    changing to orange and red

Hiding behind shadowy trees,
    mountains and hills throughout the night

Another photo of the Coachella valley's
    nighttime skies
No two photos are quite the same,
    each bringing brand new sighs
Beauty is in the eye of the beholder,
    thanks to God's creation
Thank God we Americans can enjoy
    this great beautiful nation

IT TOOK ME MANY YEARS TO LET GO.
I FINALLY LET GO AND IT WAS TOO LATE..

A poem inspired by a suggestion from Janice Parham Jesson

It took me many years to let go.
    I finally let go and it was too late..
Then I opened my eyes and then said no
    I will face my past and on with the show

So many years passed on by, with no hope in sight
    Until I faced my fears and stood up to the fight
I thought it was too late, but life is still up ahead
    I can accomplish anything before I am dead

It took me many years to finally let go
    I let go and thought it was too late for the show
Then I woke up from the pain and started to write with this gift
    I didn't know I had, until God blessed me with this shift
From stressed filled thoughts of despair and desperation
    I think God again for living in this great nation

It is never too late to start over again and just let go
      The past is the past, the future is up ahead
There is so much we can do before we wind up dead
      Decisions we made in the past can become such a show
If instead of dwelling on them, we move forward instead
      And live life to its fullest whether real high or real low

Take the good with the bad,
stop looking back at the pain
If you do not, the thoughts will drive you insane
The past is over, up ahead the future
is waiting for you
Stop kicking yourself, look up ahead,
what will you do

IF I COULD ONLY WRITE, I WOULD WRITE YOU A SONG

A Poem inspired by a suggestion from Debbie Gatlin

If I could only write, I would write you a song
It might be too short, but may also be too long
It might be about love; I might make you sad
It's a gift from God, and might make you glad
If I could write, I would write you a song
It might be weak, but I think it could be strong
My gift from God is the poem, easy for me
It has to be God's gift as you can see
If I could write, I would write you a song
About friendships and the past before they are gone
Memories forever in your brain to retrieve anytime
This is my wish, my poems to stop
your thoughts on a dime
Remember these words, as simple as a suggestion
Then I start to write and never
second guess the question
As you can see, rhymes are easy, rhymes are free
Rhymes can make a song, for the whole world to see
If I could write, I would write you a song
I hope you love it, when I finish, I feel so strong
Even if you don't, I will continue to write
Because if I stop,
the world would lose a beautiful sight

CANCER TOOK THE LOVE OF MY LIFE

    A Poem inspired by a suggestion from
    Eric Huttar

Cancer took the love of my life
The pain cuts through my brain just like a knife
She was the first that showed me
    what true Godly love was
This will be my last love song to her because
She is the best, she fought till the end,
    I will never forget
Until we meet again in heaven,
    your memories I will let
Roam in my head, and also in my thoughts
    I will release
And continue to tell the world about her love
    she had with such ease
She says this world, she was just passing through
She fought the good fight, forever I will love her,
    that is what I will do
Hospice told me today, she has only less than a week
If this is true, and she leaves this earth
    I will continue to seek
For answers, memories, until I see her again
    up in heaven
We have been together a short time;
    the years were only seven
But it seems like a lifetime,
    as she kept the faith in this fight

There's a crown of righteousness in heaven,
> she'll welcome the sight
It's laid up for her,
> waiting for her to enter from the Lord
I know once she enters, she will never be bored
I love Deb with my heart forevermore, I cannot wait
Until I join her up in heaven
> at the beloved pearly gate

THE EARTH CRIES OUT FOR HUMANITY

A Poem inspired by a suggestion from Ntwanano Mashele

The earth cries out for humanity
To be a bit more kind with reality
Stop the violence, stop the pollution
Stop the waste and all the commotion
The earth cries out for humanity
With earthquakes, plagues, floods; can't you see
There is only one earth, it may not be here forever
So, humanity needs to take care of it together
The earth cries out for humanity
So, we can all live in peace and tranquility
Will mankind change, or is it too late
Will the earth fight back and become too irate?
The earth cries out for humanity
To be more kind, with each other, don't you agree
Instead of living selfish lives,
      we must all come together
I know we can do it, in any kind of weather
The earth cries out for humanity
Through drought, famine, and poverty
We all must elect leaders who have good intentions
Or else the earth may fight back in every direction
The earth cries out for humanity
If you are not crying too, then you do not see
That the end is near, and too much is at stake
For all humanity can end, the future is ours to make.

IF ALL POETS WROTE THE SAME WHAT BORING POEMS THEY WOULD BE

A poem inspired by a suggestion by Lance Armstrong-Robinson

If all poets wrote the same
What boring poems they would be
Sometimes people say mine are a little lame
I think they're all barking up the wrong tree

Not all rhymes are the same,
not all poets are quite equal
I am a simple poet;
my endings aren't the same as their prequel
I'm trying to stretch my ability
when it comes to God's little gift
So, when I write another poem, all I want to do is lift
Everybody's spirit and mood up into the air
So, then everyone can forget about their past
and of their past despair
This has always been my purpose in all of my writings
So when you read my poetry books,
in your brain will be the sightings
Of love, pain, hurt from the past,
and a few more blessings in disguise
I will continue to write,
and sit back and wait for everyone's sighs.

Not all poets write with the same ability and style
But, when I write, all I want in return
is a simple little smile
From everyone's faces as you turn the pages
                        of my book
I hope I took you places, in the back
                        of your brains hidden nook
Please just tell all your friends about
this poet you know named Claus
And hopefully all my books will be
on your coffee table in your house
Maybe by the year's end,
I should have at least four books published
With so many of my poems,
I hope your pain will be squished
As you read my books
because I am like no other poet or writer
And because of this,
I know our future will be forever brighter

MY GIFT FROM GOD
THE POEM AND WRITING

My gift from God has to be the poem and writing
Because they come out so natural
      and fast like lightning
Poems and writing are like breathing to me
Once I sit down, out comes another two or three

My gift from God, is poetry for the whole world to see
When I get finished writing,
      I can't believe they came from me
The gift has to be from God,
      because Satan would not allow
For me to express love, beauty and emotion
      and to see the WOW

My gift from God comes with the love
      to write with a rhyme
With poems and messages,
      hidden in the paragraphs and lines
From my brain unto the page,
      the keystrokes pushing through
Telling different stories,
      while still rhyming they will do

My gift from God,
    sometimes I don't give enough credit
Because I know I am not writing this,
    the glory is all his
God from up above inspires my creativity
With words that release me out of the world's insanity

My gift from God, the poem is my specialty
Didn't know he gave me this gift,
    but I know now it is reality
The love to write is more love
    than anything else in this earth
I must embrace this gift,
    and let my life have a new rebirth

My gift from God is to write words
    for the whole world to see
My words and poems are my purpose in life,
    don't you agree
I didn't really start writing until age 36,
    I was just too blind to see
Working stupid dead-end jobs,
    I never liked which made me too busy

LOW SELF ESTEEM

Low self-esteem is something I have always had
I don't remember being happy, I just remember sad
I don't want anybody's pity, I just want some respect
For my God given ability to write even if you reject
My simple rhymes which to me are my gift
Some just think they are forced,
    but these words I just lift
Out of my simple mind,
    and out of my simple vocabulary
And write them down and
    hope people think they're extraordinary

Low self-esteem, I don't know where it came from
But I bet it had something to do
    with people calling me dumb
Sometimes others would just treat me
    with such disrespect
Then it made it hard to make friends,
    and a wall I would erect
Around my heart, around my soul,
    around my entire life
Until one day I got a job and met my beautiful wife

No marriage is perfect, and neither is ours,
    we've had our share
Of ups and downs,
    then we had a daughter and boys we had a pair
They are all grown up now, they grew up so fast
As I look back now, I feel bad about the past

So many mistakes, so many miscalculations
    and so many actions
We all wish we could go back
    and change our own reactions
These rhymes are so simple,
    but they are from God and from me
I thank God again for the United States
    where my speech is forever free
To express my feelings, whether about love,
    suicidal thoughts or hate
I know some of my rhymes are simple,
    but some are really great
So, if you like what you read
    and want to participate in my journey
You can be a part of a future book,
    with a suggestion, simple as can be
I will take your suggestion
    and turn it into another beautiful work of art
All you have to do is make a suggestion
    and wait, then I will start
Exploring my simple brain,
    start writing with such ease
Out will come a beautiful poem,
    and I know it will please

MAKING NEW FRIENDS EVERY SINGLE DAY

Making new friends every single day
Is what happens in such unusual ways
From waking up and checking on Facebook
To going shopping or marketing my new book

Everyday a new person comes along just like birth
From a different state or country around the earth
Sometimes I get inspired by their story,
    then I have to write
Another poem so the world can experience
    a brand-new sight

They could be from Pakistan, England or Nigeria
Or just another state or city like Peoria
They may know someone who knows
    someone else who knows
So and so, who lives in faraway places
    like where it snows

A stranger is just an unmet friend
    we meet along the way
Of life just like driving around
    from the mountain to the bay
We can meet on messenger, some asking for money
Or some we can meet outside
    where it is way too sunny

Wherever we meet them, we can,
>   with our message send
What needs to be said all we need to do is just bend
our self-comfort zone, so we can meet another
person so close, they will feel like a sister or a brother

It could be on Instagram and someone had a dream
just the night before,
>   how strange it was about my name
Gods coincidence and purpose for our life
Can be reinforced like cutting a cake with a knife

WHAT DOES IT FEEL LIKE TO BE NUMBER ONE?

What does it feel like to be number one?
To shine so bright just like the sun
What does it feel like to be the best?
In any situation, no matter the quest
Is it so wrong to shoot for the stars?
Perhaps pass the moon and end up on mars
Striving and thirsting, always trying to be better
With all your emotions writing more greater
Each and every day, as soon as you wake
Inside your brain, words causing an earthquake
Each new day bringing a brand-new surprise
As others read your words, you can feel the sighs
Stop worrying about others, just be yourself
Don't waste your day with your life on the shelf
Get up and go until you cannot any longer
If you do, your life with be so much stronger
While reading, writing or helping others
    all along the way
Each one of us really do have so much to say
We all have a story that needs to be told
Write them down, put in a book, then they can be sold
Don't put it off until tomorrow
Write down your happiness and even your sorrow
Write down the in between moments about your life
Write about vacations, fights, family
    and of course the strife

HOW DO I MAKE MONEY WITH MY WORDS?

How do I make money with my words?
It's like asking to fly with neighborhood birds
Seems impossible, too much competition
I guess I will just write and continue my wishing
That others will love the words that I write
No matter how simple complicated or trite
I will continue to deliver them for you all
To read throughout the pages of books in the mall
Hopefully soon this country will reopen
And I can do book signings because it has been
So stupid and unnecessary for a virus and the clowns
To force the whole world to close everyone down
For a virus with a ninety eight percent
chance of survival
So, what is really going on
with the situation of betrayal
Fear mongering from media,
doctors and such political lies
It is time to make money, open up now,
listen to our cries
We all need to get on with our lives,
because it has been
Too long already, its unnatural to stay home again
Away from our jobs, or businesses, because we need
To make money and pay all our bills,
that's the American creed
To follow our dreams, happiness
and our desires and love
All of our works and working
is a gift from God above

DOES THE WORLD REALLY NEED ANOTHER POET?

Does the world really need another poet?
Do you have the gift and just don't know it?
I didn't know until I was thirty-five
I have written so much now; I feel so alive

Kept putting off this powerful gift from God
The words are the grass, my brain is the sod
All 300 poems sitting in my computer for 20 years
Until one day, put them together without any fears

About if people didn't like them, I just don't care
All I know is that I had to organize and share
I did not separate the good from the bad
I did not separate the happy from the sad

This gift from God has been lying dormant
For twenty years in my computer, it is time to cement
All the poems into books for the whole world to see
They are for everyone, once you read, you will agree

Does the world really need another poet?
The answer is yes, I bet you didn't know it
I am just one amongst millions you see
Poems are for you and poems are from me

CLAUS IN THE HOUSE

My name is Claus, it rhymes with house
I don't have a mouse, I don't wear a blouse
And I ain't no louse,
I love to write, my words are quite
A beautiful sight, no need to fight
My feelings which are right, because they just might
Fill your brain and excite, as you read in the night

Poems are from me, so you can see
The gift inside of me, just like leaves in a tree
Blowing in the breeze, my rhymes will just freeze
Anytime that you tease, and I will not be pleased
When you make fun of my name, my life is no game
So, in return I will tame, your words which are lame
So, think next time, I write another simple rhyme
And your thoughts stop on a dime
To some hate speech is a crime

Think next time you choose to bully
Or harass others your thoughts you need to fully
Understand the pain you may inflict
On others with words that contradict
The person you are making fun of
Instead you need to ask forgiveness from up above
from the Lord to repent and instead send love
to everyone you have ever hurt in your past
maybe then your victim's lives can become a blast
and all of the pain will never again last
the misery inflicted on others
will forever be in the past

THE MORE I WRITE

The more I write, the happier I get
As I sit and think, my emotions I will let
Go unto the page, in sentences and rhymes
This is much better than committing some crimes
I write about writing because I love it so much
Nothing else in the world has ever brought me such
Happy emotions inside my brain that I release
Unto the page in rhymes with such an ease
The more I write, more thoughts come right through
With each simple rhyme, nothing else I want to do
I hope I am not too repetitive with each new verse
This writing is a gift from God,
      I no longer think it's a curse
I thought before while I tried to sleep night after night
Suffering insomnia,
      words in my brain were such a sight
Once I woke up and wrote the words down
My face turned to a smile from an unhappy frown
Such a release, I never appreciated the gift
The year 2000 went by
      and disappeared with such swift
Emotions and energy, forgotten until recently
Went through all my poems,
      now my book's finally free
This gift is still alive in my brain, I thank God again
So now I have many more poems,
      more books to begin
Sifting and sorting through folders
      in my computer until
I sort out my compiled poems,
      and bookshelves you will fill

With another brand-new book, from little ole me
Won't take too much longer, believe me, you will see
Another couple of months,
    who knows how many books I'll release
Because this gift from God
controls me and the world will be pleased

GOD ALMIGHTY

You are God almighty
Lord and savior to us all
If we all will just open our eyes
Then we all can see
All of your glory
And all of your righteousness
The bibles full of your story
And all of your graciousness
He is God almighty
Master of the universe
From continents to all the seas
As we read verse to verse
The bible and the words within
Are for all to read and share
If you believe in Jesus, you will win
If not, you lose and live in despair
Believe and accept Jesus as lord right now
You do not want to miss out on the savior
Life comes right at you as it will plough
Before it's over, it's time to change your behavior
Before It's too late and the rapture comes
It will come before you know it
Eat up the word, and don't leave any crumbs
Soon we will die, where will your soul end up
If up in heaven with the lord,
we must drink of his cup
Receive his salvation, repent of all our sins
Then our lives will have meaning,
then our new life begins

Claus Ranswill is a Christian, father of 3 children, husband of 28 years to wife Debra , writer, and life insurance agent. He is an entrepreneur and he has a tremendous love for writing and this book is the second in a series full of poems written between 2000-2003. Claus has written over 400 poems including some written since his first book God Only Knows was published in June 2020.

Claus has written over 100 news stories for his college newspaper back in 2000-2003. He has also written a screenplay, a children's book in need of an illustrator, numerous short stories and many other writings which will be published in the near future. He continues to write new poems almost every day and will need to continue publishing books to keep up with his writing. Claus loves to get feedback from all his readers whether positive or negative.

Made in the USA
Middletown, DE
02 September 2020

17065555R00073